REMEMBERING REMUS IN PRICE HILL

Julie Hotchkiss ◆ Joyce Meyer

Published by Edgecliff Press

in partnership with the
Price Hill Historical Society & Museum

Cincinnati, Ohio

George Remus, Price Hill's Bootlegger King

Remembering Remus in Price Hill

By Julie Hotchkiss & Joyce Meyer

Published by Edgecliff Press, LLC.,
and the Price Hill Historical Society & Museum
Cincinnati, Ohio

www.edgecliffpress.com
www.pricehill.org

ISBN Number 978-0-9839486-0-5

Book design: Julie Hotchkiss

Front cover photo (door knocker): Creative Commons/Vidalia 11_Karen
Front cover photo (marble): © Walter S. Arnold, Stonecarver.com
Back cover photo (George Remus): Courtesy of the Delhi Historical Society

Internal photographs are from the collection of the Price Hill Historical Society & Museum or public domain images, unless otherwise indicated. The Delhi Historical Society graciously gave permission to reproduce may of the photographs from their Remus collection and their photographs are credited in the pages of this book.

10   9   8   7   6   5   4   3   2   1

Published in the United States of America

Price Hill's Bootlegger King

At the Price Hill Historical Society, we are often asked questions about a famous, or rather infamous, person who briefly made Price Hill his home. No, not Jerry Springer, but George Remus, a lifelong teetotaler who is renowned as the "King of the Bootleggers."

Almost a century after George Remus operated one of the most extensive bootlegging operations in the country during Prohibition, his name still has the ability to conjure up images of sleek automobiles, gilt-edged mansions, and other Jazz Age excesses.

Why is the story of Remus so fascinating to so many people? Perhaps F. Scott Fitzgerald was the man to answer that question. Remus is thought to have been the inspiration for Fitzgerald's most well-known novel, *The Great Gatsby*. There are definite connections between the two men: Fitzgerald lived in Louisville, Kentucky, for a time, and Remus's business in the Midwest certainly took him to Louisville.

Remus met one of his best customers, Al Capone, at a bar called the Rookwood Rathskeller in the Seelbach Hotel in Louisville. Fitzgerald was also often found whiling away his leisure hours at the Rathskeller, and he would have heard about the infamous "King of the Bootleggers" while he was there.

In fact, a former Rathskeller bartender named Max Allen, Jr., once recalled in an interview that there was a photograph hanging behind the bar of Al Capone, George

Remus, the mayor of Louisville, the city's police chief, and F. Scott Fitzgerald. No one can find that old photograph, but the similarities between the fictional social-climbing bootlegger that Fitzgerald installed as the central character of his greatest novel and the life of George Remus are evident in the lavish lifestyles both enjoyed, as well as the sudden fall from glory that both suffered.

And certainly Remus's fall was as dramatic as his rise had been; it was the sort of story that has been providing provocative plots for as long as people have been writing fiction. Indeed, the story of George Remus and what occurred during the time he lived in Price Hill owes as much to tall tales and rumors as it does to the truth.

We'll try to separate the life of one of the most notorious figures of the Prohibition era from the legends that surround him, but we'll provide the legends, too—in the features titled "Remus Memories" throughout this book.

Some of the stories about George Remus are just too good not to pass on, and if they were good enough for Fitzgerald to incorporate into his novel, they're good enough for us . . . so sit back and enjoy the life and legend of Price Hill's own "King of the Bootleggers."

Remus Before
Price Hill

George Remus (front row center) as a schoolboy in Chicago, c. 1890

Photo Courtesy of the Delhi Historical Society

George Remus was born in Germany on November 13, probably in the year 1878. That is the date on his death certificate and his grave marker, but in other records the year is variously given as 1874 and 1876. He immigrated with his family to Chicago when he was very young, in about 1883. His father was sick or disabled, and George had to work to support his family from an early age. He went to work as a pharmacist's assistant when he was about 14. By the time he was 19, he was so successful that he owned the pharmacy. There were rumors that he actually forced his uncle, who had opened the store originally, to sell it to him. This may be the first sign of his single-minded personality when it came to getting what he wanted.

Remus continued to prosper, and when he was 24, he bought a second drugstore. He had also found time to study law, pass the bar, and become a practicing attorney in Chicago just after the turn of the century. (Some sources say he was self-taught, others that he graduated from the Illinois College of Law.) He married his first wife, Lillian, about this time, and they had a daughter named Romola in April 1900.

Remus was apparently very successful as a lawyer,

George Remus, in about 1920

REMUS MEMORIES

Johnny Gehrum was one of George Remus's trusted lieutenants. He built a large house on Queen City Avenue, directly across the street from Death Valley, where Remus's bootlegging operation was headquartered. The house sat on a high knob, surrounded by a large swath of property. Oreste Barroni, one of Gehrum's son-in laws, kept horses in stables near Gehrum's house.

Sometime in the late forties, Gehrum had the house remodeled and created four apartments. There was one for each of his daughters and their husbands, one for his son and his wife and daughter, and one for himself. About the time Roy Hotchkiss married his wife Gini, Gehrum's daughter Ada and her husband moved out. Ada was a friend of Gini's mother, so they managed to get the apartment and lived there for a few years; it was where their daughter Julie was born. It was a pretty wacky place to live. They went to the third birthday party of Gehrum's granddaughter, and her present was brought into the kitchen—a pony named Snowball that promptly ate the birthday cake. Then Oreste Barroni got tired of cutting the grass so he bought a couple of goats. One of the goats soon killed one of Barroni's horses, so Oreste had to go back to cutting the grass himself. Of course there were rumors of tunnels that ran from the house under Queen City Avenue over to Death Valley (page 14). Whenever Mr. Gehrum would go out, Roy would go down the cellar and look for the tunnel. He never found it, but the cellar was rather odd. There were shelves from top to bottom along all the walls. They were filled with glass jars of all sizes. Maybe Mr. Gehrum thought if Prohibition returned and he had to start making moonshine again, he would have something to put it in.

specializing in criminal defense law. He successfully represented the defendants in several murder trials, and by 1920, he had been practicing law for twenty years in the Chicago courts and was earning $50,000 a year—the equivalent of more than a million dollars annually today.

Although the murder suspects Remus "got off" brought him notoriety, there was another class of criminal defendants that interested him. These were the Chicago-area

Bootleg whiskey ready for transport during Prohibition

bootleggers who were flaunting the law after the passage of
the 18th Amendment—Prohibition—in January 1920. When
Remus saw some of his clients grow wealthy supplying
whiskey to the thirsty masses, he decided to study the
Volstead Act, which Congress had passed to enforce the
18th Amendment. He was looking for loopholes that would
allow him to make big money, too.

Remus discovered that the Volstead Act allowed the
sale of alcohol legally for medicinal purposes. He already
owned pharmacies, so he began to buy up distilleries as
well, with the idea that most of the stock he produced as
medicine would "disappear" between the distilleries and
the pharmacies. Instead, it would find its way to the more
lucrative black market in illegal whiskey that had sprung up
all over the country after Prohibition took effect.

When he contemplated how to get his new product to
customers, Remus decided that transportation was one
of the most important aspects of successful bootlegging.

His move to Cincinnati was completely calculated: he recognized that the city was more centrally located than Chicago. In fact, it was located within a few hundred miles of every major distillery producing bonded whiskey in the United States, including the ones he had purchased.

One of the distilleries he owned, the Fleischmann Company, was actually located in Cincinnati. The city was also in a good central location for distribution routes that could easily reach most of the major metropolitan areas in the eastern half of the country.

So in 1920, George Remus made the decision to leave behind his successful law practice in Chicago for a new "extralegal" career in Cincinnati. He had divorced his wife Lillian that same year, apparently because he had taken up with Augusta Imogene Brown Holmes, known as Imogene, a former delicatessen worker who had become his secretary.

REMUS MEMORIES

As George and Imogene Remus celebrated the opening of the beautiful swimming pool at their Price Hill home (shown on page 20), the buzz of the guests' conversation filled the night air, and so did the music of Gus Schmitz's Band. Remus relished the fact that he could display his wealth in front of his friends and acquaintances by lavishing them with gifts. The band was no exception—the musicians were given diamond stickpins to wear in the lapels of their tuxedos while they performed. A highlight of the evening was showing off of the newly built Grecian swimming pool. As the story goes, Gus (banjo) and the other band members were asked by Remus to "take a swim." They jumped into the water wearing their tuxedos and the expensive gift pins. (Ladies in attendance were provided with bathing suits!) Fortunately, Gus Schmitz's pin (page 11) as well as the story of the party have been preserved all these years.

Imogene and her daughter Ruth accompanied him to Cincinnati, and George Remus and Imogene Brown were married on June 26, 1920, in Newport, Kentucky.

Then the newlyweds were ready to find a place to live in Cincinnati, after which Remus lost no time setting up a lucrative, if illegal, bootlegging operation in the city.

Imogene Remus

Photo Courtesy of the Delhi Historical Society

REMUS MEMORIES

William Doolan, known as Bill, arranged and decorated bouquets and florals for Edward A. Forter, a florist on Fourth Street in Cincinnati. Bill began working for the florist when he was about 14 years old, and he remembers that on one occasion, Imogene Remus phoned for flowers to decorate the long arbor that led to the pool at their Price Hill estate. But when the flowers arrived, Imogene wanted more.

The Remus mansion had a large porch, which George had screened in to house his plants. Photos of the pool area show pot after pot of greenery. This couple loved plants and lots of them. So, when George heard of Imogene's disappointment, he promptly said to young Bill, who had remained to decorate the arbor after the delivery truck left, "Go get more flowers!" Doolan also remembered other parties where the city's police chief, mayor, and other politicians left with bottles of whiskey tucked under their arms.

A Mansion
on the Hill

At top, the Hermosa Avenue house in Price Hill where Imogene and
George Remus lived from 1920 to 1925; below, the home's solarium

By the time he arrived in Cincinnati in 1920, George Remus was already quite wealthy. One of the first things he did was purchase a grand mansion at 825 Hermosa Avenue, on the southwest corner of Hermosa and West Eighth in Price Hill. The house had originally belonged to Cincinnati beer baron Henry Lackmann. The building sat far back from the street, surrounded by acres of property, and could not be seen easily by passers-by — perhaps one of the features that drew Remus to the estate.

Although the house was already large and luxurious, Remus set about remodeling it. He added a wing with an indoor swimming pool at a reported cost of $100,000. A magazine of the time described the fixtures in the bathrooms as made of solid gold; they were probably gold plate, but were nonetheless ostentatious. The magazine story also mentioned a gold piano, and the photographs of the mansion's interior that accompanied the story showed that no expense was spared to make the house a showplace. Apparently there were also barns on the property, housing horses that were a source of fascination to the young boys in the neighborhood.

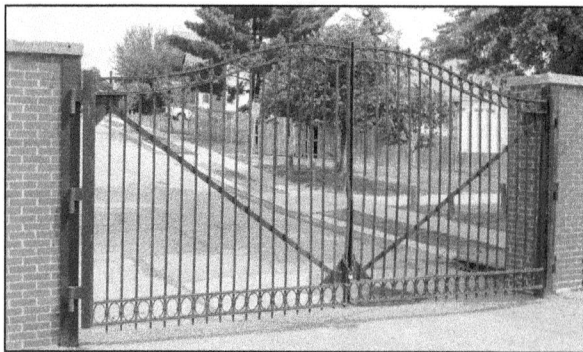

The gates from the Remus estate in Price Hill, now the back gates of Elder High School

The wrought iron gates that once guarded the Hermosa Avenue entrance of the Remus property are still in Price Hill. They now serve

REMUS MEMORIES

The Remus estate was surrounded by a fence that had several entrances, marked by pillars and wrought iron gates. Though the place was well protected, on occasion those gates would open to welcome guests to George and Imogene's grand parties at the mansion. The lavish living did not continue after the fall of the bootleg baron, however. With his possessions lost or sold, George Remus's home was to be torn down in the mid 1930s. One source has told us that a certain Father Krusling sent a delegate to the property at Eighth and Hermosa Avenue and secured the wrought iron fence and gates for the entrance to Elder High School, and the gates were installed on the school grounds. While there has been some discrepancy as to which gates these are, we believe that the gates in question (shown in the photograph on the previous page) still stand at the entrance to Elder located at the end of Iliff Avenue, now renamed Panther Court.

as the back gates at nearby Elder High School, located on Panther Court (formerly Iliff Avenue).

One of the oft-told tales that surrounds Remus's life in Price Hill concerns a New Year's Eve party in 1922. According to the story, George and Imogene Remus threw a soiree for one hundred wealthy society folk, and at dawn, each woman at the party was given keys to a new motorcar for the drive home. There were also rumors of party favors that included pearl necklaces and other extravagances, but the recipients of any such lavish gifts are all long gone now. The diamond stickpin in the photograph at right, however, is one bit of evidence of the gifts Remus distributed

This diamond stickpin was presented to Gus Schmitz, a musician who played at one of Remus's extravagant parties

as he tried to become part of the city's social hierarchy.

He was also apparently generous with government officials at every level, offering substantial bribes to hundreds of policemen,

Remus (seated at center) gathered with some of his cohorts at the Cottage Tavern (now the Sunset Pub) in Price Hill, not far from his home on Hermosa Avenue

judges, and high-level appointees, including $500,000 to the U.S. attorney general in Warren Harding's administration. At the height of his success in the bootleg business, Remus is said to have employed 3,000 people and spent $20 million in bribes—but his bootlegging profits have been estimated at anywhere from $45 to $75 million.

Death Valley "ranch" was a compound of buildings southwest of Lick Run (now Queen City Avenue) where Remus had his bootlegging operation in the 1920s

REMUS MEMORIES

Larry Schmolt had an uncle who was a small-time bootlegger who got the whiskey he delivered to customers from George Remus. Every Sunday he would call up his sister, Larry's mother, to tell her he was going to take the family for a ride. Larry's dad worked on the railroad and was usually out of town on Sundays, and the family didn't have a car of their own. So that Sunday ride was an exciting part of the week, and when their uncle showed up, Larry and his sister and mother would be dressed in their Sunday best, ready for a nice ride in the big Buick. Larry was only about three years old, sitting in his mother's lap in the front seat, but he remembers that the first stop was always a farm on Queen City Avenue, where his uncle would hop out and open the trunk, at which point some men would come out of the barn and load boxes in the trunk. Then the Buick would take off again, by all appearances just a nice family out for a Sunday drive, stopping to visit "friends." They'd make the rounds of many different houses in the area, and at each stop, Larry's uncle would go to the trunk, get out a box, and carry it up to the house. The next morning when Larry's dad got home, he would ask what they family did on Sunday and his wife would tell him about her brother taking them for a ride. Mr. Schmolt, knowing his brother-in-law was a bootlegger, would be furious. "He's going to get all of you killed!" he'd say, but Larry just thought his dad considered his uncle to be a bad driver. He didn't learn the truth of what was at that farm—Death Valley—until he was a teenager and heard people talking about Remus and his bootlegging operation.

George Remus lived in Price Hill during his brief bootlegging career in the 1920s, but his base of operations for bootlegging was a large, barren area with several barns and buildings on Lick Run (now Queen City Avenue) known as "Death Valley" (diagram on page 14).

Death Valley was located near where Gehrum Lane runs off Queen City today. Like the property where Remus's mansion once stood, the Death Valley "ranch" was developed in later years into residences, in this case a large apartment complex called Four Towers Apartments.

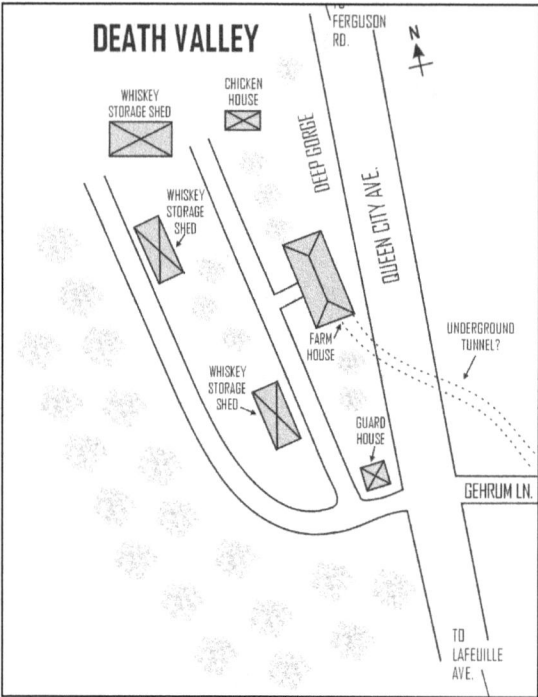

DEATH VALLEY

FERGUSON RD.

N

WHISKEY STORAGE SHED

CHICKEN HOUSE

DEEP GORGE

WHISKEY STORAGE SHED

QUEEN CITY AVE.

FARM HOUSE

UNDERGROUND TUNNEL?

WHISKEY STORAGE SHED

GUARD HOUSE

GEHRUM LN.

TO LAFEUILLE AVE.

Gehrum Lane was named for Remus's business associate, Johnny Gehrum, who built a large house for himself, complete with his own swimming pool and stables, on a high spot just across from Death Valley. He and his family lived there for many years. In the 1950s, the house was divided into apartments, where several members of the Gehrum family continued to live until it was razed and replaced with a new apartment building in the 1960s.

There were reports of a tunnel under the road at Death Valley, for quick getaways. Like every other aspect of Remus's operation, the layout was organized to work efficiently and effectively in his bootlegging empire.

The site of Death Valley today—a large, multi-building apartment complex was built on the site decades ago

14

The Bootleg Kingdom

Photo Courtesy of the Delhi Historical Society

Above, a gathering of guests for a dinner party George and Imogene gave in 1920; at right, a diagram of the grounds of their grand estate in Price Hill

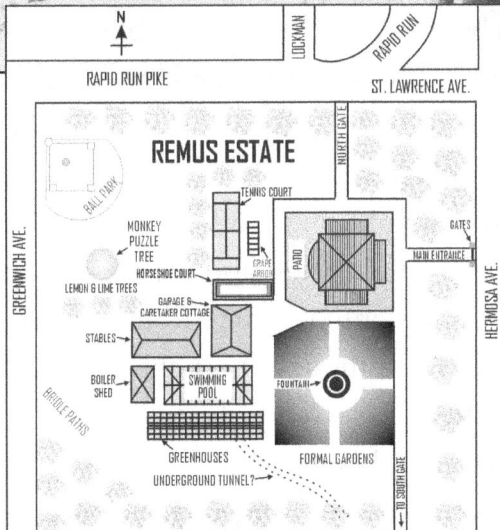

N

RAPID RUN PIKE

LOCKMAN

RAPID RUN

ST. LAWRENCE AVE.

REMUS ESTATE

BALL PARK

NORTH GATE

TENNIS COURT

GATES

MONKEY PUZZLE TREE

GREENWICH AVE.

GRAPE ARBOR

PATIO

MAIN ENTRANCE

HORSESHOE COURT

LEMON & LIME TREES

HERMOSA AVE.

GARAGE & CARETAKER COTTAGE

STABLES

BOILER SHED

SWIMMING POOL

FOUNTAIN

BRIDLE PATHS

GREENHOUSES

FORMAL GARDENS

TO SOUTH GATE

UNDERGROUND TUNNEL?

Remus was successful as a bootlegger because he had a vertical lock on the industry—his distilleries made the whiskey (for medicinal purposes, as far as the revenue men were concerned), and he also operated a fleet of trucks that delivered the product to cities in the Midwest and South. Keeping the trucks running was vital, and more than one repair garage around Price Hill made good money working on those trucks. The Ford dealership on Glenway at Beech Avenue, across from Mt. St. Vincent Academy (now Seton High School), was one of the places where the Remus fleet was serviced.

The building that housed a Ford dealership at Glenway & Beech in the 1920s is still standing today

George Remus also had an interest in making sure there were places where the whiskey could be sold directly to the public, in bold defiance of Prohibition. These were sometimes called "blind pigs"—the notion being that advertising an attraction such as a blind pig would alert those in the know that liquor was being served without tipping off the authorities. They were also known as speakeasies, and the backbar in the Mt. Adams Bar & Grill reputedly came from a speakeasy associated with Remus, although there are no records to attest to his ownership.

To run his bootlegging enterprise as a successful business, Remus delegated tasks to trusted lieutenants. Johnny Gehrum was one of Remus's right-hand men, and he kept the operation at Death Valley running smoothly. One of the retainers at Death Valley was a woman named Mary Hubbard, known as "Old Mother Hubbard," whose testimony Charles Taft was counting on to convict Remus in his murder trial—until she refused to testify. But we're getting ahead of the story here!

Another lieutenant in his business, William Lucking, built the house with the white stucco gatehouse that sits back from the road on Cleves Warsaw Pike near Covedale. Though not quite as grand as Remus's own estate, it is a substantial house of 4000 square feet in the style of a Swiss chalet, with acres of property that were originally paid for with bootlegging profits. There was even a finished basement decorated in a style similar to the Rathskeller Bar at the Seelbach Hotel. The house was built like a fortress

REMUS MEMORIES

The photograph on page 12 shows George Remus posing at the Cottage Tavern, 4068 West Eighth Street (now the Sunset Pub), with a group of friends (or employees?). At far right is Giuseppe (Joseph) "Peno" Salamone. Peno started out working for his father, Antonio, in a produce business in Cincinnati, but soon the desire to make more money made him strike out on his own. A promissory note written in Italian on the back of an old playbill indicates that he borrowed $2500 from his mother on May 24, 1920, to purchase a produce truck. He was living in Price Hill at the time, and he soon began to use the truck to haul whiskey for the bootlegger George Remus, a more lucrative undertaking than peddling lettuce. During the time he worked for Remus, Peno was shot in the leg, and he was known to always carry a .32 Smith and Wesson pistol. His family tried to protect his reputation by saying that his limp was the result of being shot during World War I, but he never left American soil during the war.

and that it was designed to harbor a moonshine and bootlegging business on site seems apparent; there are stories that a barn on that property was used to distill whiskey.

Lucking, so the story goes, raised pigs to cover the

This house, still standing on Western Hills Avenue, provided housing for workers at Lucking's estate

smell of the stills, and there was a hidden area under the front porch of the main house as well as enough electric service to run a factory. A white stucco house on Western Hills Avenue provided housing for Lucking's workers when the property extended that far, before it was subdivided in the early 1930s when the Tudor homes on Covedale Avenue were built.

Perhaps because of his business acumen and knowledge of the Volstead Act (and all the loopholes it provided), George Remus was never arrested or charged with bootlegging, but he was convicted in 1924 of bribing officials and evading taxes. He was sentenced to two years in a federal penitentiary near Atlanta, Georgia.

Remus's mug shots

That prison was something like a luxury hotel for its rich inmates, many of whom had been incarcerated for

REMUS MEMORIES

Tony Witsken, Jr., a Price Hill native, wanted to build a house when he returned from the service in World War II. He had heard there was land available on the old Remus estate that had not yet been built on. He discovered that the undeveloped property belonged to a man by the name of Johnny Torrio, who was living at the time in Brooklyn, New York. Johnny Torrio was apparently a notorious gangster during Prohibition, who had hired Al Capone and others to run whiskey for him. After many long-distance phone calls, Mr. Torrio finally agreed to sell the property on Delehanty Court to Tony Witsken for $1,500.

A copy of the original purchase contract dated October 3, 1955, is in the archives of the Price Hill Historical Society and Museum. What is unknown is how Torrio came to acquire the land in the first place, why he was reluctant at first to sell the property, or why he finally agreed to sell it. Perhaps he had purchased it originally hoping to find money buried by Remus, as there are stories that Imogene sold off furnishings and other items belonging to her husband when he was in prison for tax evasion, but no one seems to know what happened to the money she raised. Johnny Torrio died in 1957, not long after selling the property to Tony Witsken.

violating laws associated with Prohibition. The story is that Remus traveled to prison by private rail car, reading Dante's *Inferno* on the trip. In his prison cell, he had maid service and fresh flowers every day, if the tales told about Remus are to be believed.

Are all these accounts true? Well, there are other stories that say that Remus once filled his famous swimming pool with whiskey, and then there are those legends about the brand-new Pontiac sedans he gave as gifts. It may be that when F. Scott Fitzgerald wrote *The Great Gatsby*, he thought these details were just too unbelievable, so he toned down the excesses of the bootlegger in his book, describing only

The dedication of Remus's indoor swimming pool

Gatsby's closet full of beautiful silk shirts in every color of the rainbow. But there is one detail that Gatsby's mansion retained in common with Remus's house—the swimming pool, described in detail in Fitzgerald's novel; it also serves as a symbol of what Gatsby wanted but never achieved, and of course it is the location of his death.

The photo at the top of this page shows the guests Remus and his wife invited to a party for the dedication of their own sumptuous indoor pool. They all gathered in the pool for the photograph, with

A piece of tile from the swimming pool was found in the yard of a home near where Remus's mansion once stood

20

REMUS MEMORIES

So much has been said about the Grecian swimming pool George Remus built adjacent to his Price Hill mansion. It was one of the defining details of the property, and many of the stories point to the pool as the main example of the way Remus flaunted his wealth—and shared it, as there are also stories about kids in the neighborhood being allowed to swim in the pool when Remus no longer lived there. (One story says that "Old Mother Hubbard" and Mrs. Gehrum from Death Valley served as caretakers for the estate while Remus was on trial, and they charged the boys in the neighborhood a dime each to swim in the pool.)

There are more photographs of the swimming pool than of the house itself, including photos showing the pool before and after it was filled with water. Unfortunately, none of the photographs are in color, so it's hard to imagine how elegant the pool really looked in its prime.

But in the late 1960s, a young teenage boy living on Delehanty Court (off Ridgeview Avenue) unearthed a portion of the pool's tile while removing a fence post in his father's yard. Although the yard was not the actual location of the pool, this property as well as other lots were excavated when the Remus house was razed and the land was bulldozed for development. Apparently parts of the pool were used as fill, as other people on Delehanty Court have also reported finding tiles from the swimming pool in their yards.

In the piece of the tile ornamentation uncovered by the boy moving the fence post, a section of concrete is covered with small marble tiles arranged in a mosaic pattern of interlocking rings of cream, gold, white, and coral. Again, the black and white photograph of the tiles does not do it justice, but there is a color photograph of this artifact on display at the Price Hill Historical Society and Museum.

Remus's dog seen lounging on the side of the pool, at top left in the photo. The pool was in a building separate from the main house, as shown in the diagram of the house and grounds on page 15.

Years later, people still talked about that swimming pool in Price Hill, and some people even found remnants of it, as the photograph on page 20 shows, when digging in the yards of the houses that sprung up in the Ridgeview subdivision that was built on Remus's former property.

F. Scott Fitzgerald published *The Great Gatsby* in 1925, while Remus was serving time in prison. In Fitzgerald's novel, Gatsby was never really accepted by the society swells he invited to parties at his mansion, but he might have had a nice life anyway, if not for a woman who did him

Remus was convicted of tax evasion in 1924 and was sent to a federal prison

wrong. In a case of life imitating art, when Remus returned from the penitentiary in Atlanta, he found that a woman had wronged him as well.

Federal agents, at left, taking Remus's men to prison: from left center to far right, Johnny Gehrum, Cliff Hubbard, Mike Carruthers, Willie Harr, and Mannie Kessler

Courtesy of the Delhi Historical Society

The Trial of
the Century

On October 6, 1927, George Remus shot and killed his estranged wife Imogene near the gazebo in Cincinnati's Eden Park

T he glory days of George Remus's "bootleg kingdom" began to fade when he went to prison for tax evasion and bribery. Upon his return, he discovered that he had been betrayed by his wife Imogene. She had apparently taken up with Franklin Dodge, the federal agent who had investigated her husband for tax fraud, and together Dodge and Imogene had sold the Fleischmann distillery as well as all the movable objects in the house on Hermosa Avenue.

One of the mysteries surrounding Remus's story is what happened to the fortune he amassed. No one even knows what happened to the money Imogene made selling the couple's assets. (She claimed to have received only $100 for the sale of the distillery.) Imogene and Dodge also tried to have Remus deported, claiming that he had never become a U.S. citizen. They were even accused of trying to hire a hit man for $15,000 to kill Remus.

When Remus was released from prison, Imogene filed for divorce. On October 6, 1927, she was on her way to court to petition for the divorce. She left the Walnut Hills hotel where she was staying with her daughter Ruth to take a taxicab downtown to court. But Remus was waiting for her in his Buick touring car and had his chauffeur follow her. A wild car chase through rush hour traffic ended in Eden

The gun Remus used to shoot his wife Imogene

Park when his car forced the taxi off the road, and Remus shot Imogene as she ran from the vehicle.

Ruth tried to persuade passing motorists to help her wounded mother, but no one assisted her until a man named Van der Raulston stopped and took both women to Bethesda Hospital on Reading Road, where Imogene Remus died in surgery.

Meanwhile, the chauffeur had left Eden Park in a hurry after the shooting, so Remus hitched a ride to the District One police station downtown and turned himself in. He claimed to have lost the gun he used to shoot Imogene in the crowds that gathered after the shooting, but local legend has it that he actually threw the gun away, and it was found the next spring by a child hunting for Easter eggs near the Eden Park gazebo.

The trial was a sensation in Cincinnati and across the nation. Remus served as his own defense attorney, and the prosecuting attorney was Charles P. Taft, a son of William Howard Taft, former United States president and at the time of the Remus trial, the presiding Chief Justice of the U.S. Supreme Court.

Remus, who never denied that he had shot his wife, first claimed justifiable homicide, but soon discovered

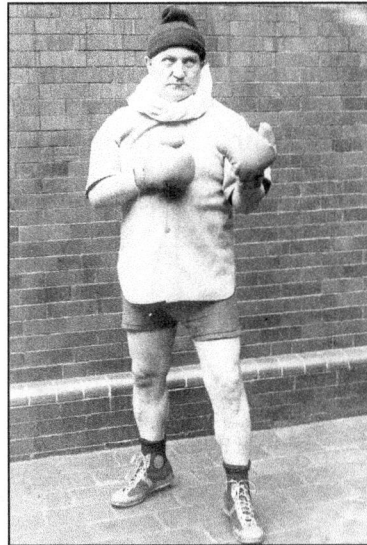

Courtesy of www.CincinnatiViews.net

Remus skillfully managed his image during the murder trial, providing the news media with "photo ops" such as this one showing him keeping in shape during the proceedings

that was not an acceptable defense in Ohio courts. So instead he claimed temporary insanity and successfully used an insanity defense for the first time in American jurisprudence.

During the trial, he vilified Imogene and her lover Franklin Dodge, telling the jury how they had looted his estate. Remus's daughter, Romola, sat next to him during the trial to lend him a bit more humanity.

Remus was well liked in Cincinnati; although, like Gatsby, he never made his way into the higher levels of society, he was charitable to the poor and generous to everyone he met. The jury deliberated only nineteen minutes before finding him not guilty on December 20, 1927. The spectators in the courtroom cheered when the verdict was read.

When he heard the verdict, Remus reportedly exclaimed, "American justice! I thank you!" One story says he threw a holiday party at the local police station later the same day for the twelve jurors who had acquitted him.

Remus thanking jurors after the murder trial

REMUS MEMORIES

During a Price Hill home tour in the 1990s, many people toured a home that had been built in 1938 on part of the former Remus estate on Hermosa Avenue. Three women who toured the home offered three different stories about Remus:

¶ The first woman said she would have starved to death if George Remus had not hired her uncle (whom she lived with) to drive a truck. Remus was the only man around with money during the Depression, she explained, and men were lucky to get work with him.

¶ The second lady remarked that her father had warned her not to go near the Remus home. So, after all those years and with her father's warning to "stay away" echoing in her ears, she had to come to see a photograph of the mansion that was on display.

¶ A third woman told how Remus had hired a relative of hers who later died in crossfire while driving a truck loaded with whiskey beneath the fruits and vegetables that appeared to be the cargo. She scolded, "You are making Remus out to be a hero, but he was a criminal!"

Whether he was judged to be a hero or a criminal, Remus's short time in Price Hill made an impression on his neighbors and created memories that lingered for many, many years with residents of the area.

Some people say that Charles Taft's political career never really recovered from the prosecution's loss at this trial. Although he had a 96 percent success rate trying cases in Hamilton County, Taft's political fortunes stalled when he lost what was billed as the "Trial of the Century." Taft remained in

Charles P. Taft

Courtesy of Delhi Historical Society

Cincinnati, serving as mayor of the city from 1955 to 1957 and as a city councilman through the 1960s and 1970s. Taft was a popular local figure, but George Remus's successful insanity plea may have played a large part in keeping the president's son from seeking higher office himself.

REMUS MEMORIES

When Colonel James Hausman was young, he lived on Ridgeview Avenue. Jim once told a story about how he and his friends would hang around the gated sandstone pillars that guarded the entrance to George Remus's estate. Many times, they would wait for the chauffeur to arrive in a long, luxurious Buick with his well-known passenger in the rear seat. Remus would roll down his window and flip a quarter with his thumb to each waiting boy. Looking out for Mr. Remus to arrive back home on Hermosa Avenue became a regular event, because the boys could always count on his generosity.

Later, Jim Hausman, a 1934 graduate of Elder High School, would write verse for a column called "When I Was a Boy" in the Cincinnati *Enquirer*. Jim also served as an advisor to General Dwight D. Eisenhower during World War II. Imagine Remus's surprise when—if ever—he found out that one of the boys who stood at his gate waiting for a quarter to fly through the air so many years earlier grew up to become a colleague of a wartime leader and future president. Jim died in 2000 in Indianapolis, Indiana.

Remus's "Third Act"

At top, the corner of West Eighth and Hermosa Avenue as it appears today; below, the house that is located now near what was the main entrance to the Remus estate on Hermosa

Scott Fitzgerald famously said that "there are no second acts in American lives." But George Remus, possibly his inspiration for Jay Gatsby, proved him wrong in that regard. If Remus's first act was as a successful attorney in Chicago and his second act was amassing—and losing—a fortune as a bootlegger headquartered on the west side of Cincinnati, he was still willing to begin again, launching a third career as a real estate developer.

After being found not guilty of murder by reason of insanity, Remus was sent to a mental institution in Lima, Ohio, but he used the prosecutor's own arguments to secure his release, since he had been declared fit to be tried for murder because he was sane. He served only three months in the state asylum, and after he was released, he first made an attempt to get back into the bootlegging business that had been so lucrative for him in the early 1920s. But he discovered that the illegal whiskey industry had been taken over by violent gangsters.

Instead, he entered the real estate business, since he still owned property in Price Hill and elsewhere. He may have had some part in subdividing and developing the land around his once splendid mansion, although there are other names associated with the lots on Ridgeview and Hermosa where homes were built in the 1930s. These names include Alice and Rose Delehanty, two Kentucky sisters who had some interests in the area. (Delehanty Court, which runs off Ridgeview, was named for them.) Another name associated with the property was Blanche Watson, a woman who eventually became Remus's third wife.

The mansion was scheduled for demolition on October 1, 1934, but the city's tax department objected, because they

REMUS MEMORIES

George Remus had a daughter named Romola, born April 7, 1900, with his first wife, Lillian. Romola was also something of a celebrity. When she was eight years old, she appeared in a silent movie, singing and dancing as none other than Dorothy Gale in a filmed version of L. Frank Baum's stage show entitled "FairyLogue and Radio-Plays." This was an elaborate multimedia show that toured Midwestern and East Coast cities to promote the 1900 Baum book, *The Wonderful Wizard of Oz*. Since it was a silent movie, Romola had no lines, but she appeared with Baum himself in the film. And you probably thought that the first film portraying Dorothy was the one with Judy Garland in her blue gingham pinafore and braided locks! Romola's hand-tinted one-reel film, made in 1908, became one of the first color movies, but no prints of it remain.

Romola was paid $5 per day to perform as Dorothy and skipped school to appear in the short film. She also later traveled with Baum to appear in live FairyLogue performances. But after appearing in a few other short films made in Chicago, her career ended as the industry moved out to California, and her parents would not let her go to Hollywood to continue acting. However, she would not leave the limelight entirely, since her father, George Remus, was in the news in October 1927, defending himself against charges that he murdered his second wife, Imogene Holmes. You can just picture Romola visiting her father in his mansion in Price Hill when he moved to Cincinnati. Romola would have been about 19 years old then. She may have shared with him her love for music, although it was later that she played and taught piano, organ, and violin. She sang and danced in vaudeville and taught dance in Chicago as well; she even wrote a song called "The Romola Waltz."

In a letter that Romola wrote in 1963 to the Chicago *Tribune*, she told of walking down Michigan Avenue at age 12 with her father, who loved to take her to matinees and to her favorite restaurant. George had a collection of letters and documents in his collection that were written by Abraham Lincoln. She wrote about actually being introduced to Robert Todd Lincoln by her father one day when they were together in Chicago. As she described Remus shaking hands with the son of the sixteenth president, you get the feeling that she admired her father the way that Remus admired Abraham Lincoln. Romola died as Romola Dunlap on February 17, 1987, and is buried in Rosehill Cemetery in Chicago.

believed the property would lose value if the house were razed, and they were looking for back taxes that had not been paid.

But eventually, with many former colleagues (and perhaps a few federal agents) looking on, the house was torn down

Remus lived with his third wife, Blanche Watson, in this house in Covington until he died in 1952

to make way for new construction. The opening page of this section shows a photograph of the apartment houses that were built at the corner of West Eighth Street and Hermosa Avenue where his property was located (top), and the house on Hermosa Avenue that currently stands where the main entrance to his mansion once was located (bottom).

Before new construction obliterated his sumptuous swimming pool, Remus reportedly opened it to the neighborhood children. The Tudor-style homes along Ridgeview Avenue, on what was once the Remus estate, were built in the 1930s, a time when many houses in the Price Hill area were built, despite the Depression.

In 1941, Remus remarried; his new wife, Blanche Watson, was a former Newport nightclub owner. (In many accounts, she is referred to as his "long-time secretary," but this may have been a euphemism used at the time to describe an unmarried couple who were frequently seen in each other's company.) There is also some evidence that Blanche was a madam who owned a brothel in Newport, and court records and newspaper accounts indicate she was involved in some real estate deals associated with the former Remus property in Price Hill.

Remus and Blanche were often spotted at area race tracks (he had owned race horses in his halcyon days), though they lived in relative obscurity in Covington, Kentucky, at 1810 Greenup Street, a far cry from the Price Hill mansion where he had once resided. During his later years, Remus also maintained business offices in the Keith Building in downtown Cincinnati.

REMUS MEMORIES

In Riverside Cemetery in Falmouth, Kentucky, George Remus is buried in the family plot of his third wife, Blanche Watson Remus, who died in 1974 and is buried next to him. The grave marker stands out in the small cemetery of mostly modest headstones, because there is a sculpture of a woman attended by two other figures atop the stone, which also marks the burial place of Blanche's parents, Taylor and Belle Watson.

With all the legends surrounding Remus in life, it's not surprising that there is yet another story associated with his grave. It's been said that the sculpture was one of the few things left after Imogene sold all the contents of Remus's Price Hill mansion when he was in prison. The figures on either side in the sculpture once had wings. But someone wrote a letter to Blanche Remus, saying that

The former angels atop George Remus's grave

Remus's grave should not be guarded by angels, all things considered. The story is that Blanche, in a fit of pique, broke off the wings.

Is the story true? We don't know, but as you can see in the photograph above, the supporting statues are clearly patched on the back shoulders, just where wings once sprouted.

When George Remus died on January 20, 1952, from a cerebral hemorrhage he had suffered a few days earlier, the headline in the Cincinnati *Times-Star* read, "Another Gatsby Passes." George Remus, the King of the Bootleggers, is buried in Riverside Cemetery in Falmouth, Kentucky.

The grave of George Remus, King of the Bootleggers, in Riverside Cemetery, Falmouth, Kentucky

Bibliography

If you'd like to find out more about George Remus and the Prohibition era, we recommend the following sources.

Brunsman, Barrett J. "Queen City Inspired Fitzgerald," *Cincinnati Enquirer Sunday Magazine*, August 22, 1999.

Burns, Ken. *Prohibition.* Video, 5-part PBS television documentary. October 2011.

Coffey, Thomas M. *The Long Thirst: Prohibition in America.* New York: W. W. Norton & Company, 1975.

Cook, William A. *The King of the Bootleggers: A Biography of George Remus.* Jefferson, NC: McFarland, 2008.

The Drug Library. Website at www.druglibrary.org that includes a version of the Remus story.

Fitzgerald, F. Scott. *The Great Gatsby.* New York: Scribner, 1925/1999.

Fortrin, Roger. *One Man's Justice.* Cincinnati: Ohio Bookstore, 1990.

Holden, Craig, *The Jazz Bird* (a novel). New York: Simon & Schuster, 2002.

And plan a visit to the Price Hill Historical Society & Museum (www.pricehill.org), which has photos and information about George Remus, as well as the Delhi Historical Society (www.delhihistoricalsociety.org), where there is a collection of many photographs documenting the life and career of the "King of the Bootleggers."

Acknowledgments

The authors would like to acknowledge the assistance of the volunteer staff at the Price Hill Historical Society & Museum and Peg Schmidt at the Delhi Historical Society for their invaluable assistance in researching this book. Thanks also to the Delhi Historical Society for allowing us to use many of their photographs in this book.

In addition, a special thanks to the people who shared their own recollections of Remus in Price Hill in the "Remus Memories" sections:

Bob Doolan

Roy Hotchkiss

Larry Salamone

William Schmitz

Larry Schmolt

Marilyn Schutte

Steve Witsken

If you have a memory of George Remus or his Price Hill home, the Price Hill Historical Society would love to hear it (RememberingRemus@pricehill.org).

www.ingramcontent.com/pod-product-compliance
Lightning Source LLC
Chambersburg PA
CBHW071754020426
42331CB00008B/2309